THE OPIOID EPIDEMIC AND THE ADDICTION CRISIS

Elliott Smith

Cicely Lewis, Executive Editor

Lerner Publications ◆ Minneapolis

LETTER FROM CICELY LEWIS

Dear Reader,

I started the Read Woke challenge in response to the needs of my students. I wanted my students to read books that challenged social norms, gave voice to the voiceless, and sought to challenge the status quo. Have you ever felt as if the truth was being hidden from you? Have

Cicely Lewis

you ever felt like adults are not telling you the full story because you are too young? Well, I believe you have a right to know about the issues that are plaguing our society. I believe that you have a right to hear the truth.

I created Read Woke Books because I want you to be knowledgeable and compassionate citizens. You will be the leaders of our society soon, and you need to be equipped with knowledge so that you can treat others with the dignity and respect they deserve. And so you can be treated with that same respect.

As you turn these pages, learn about how history has impacted the things we do today. Hopefully you can be the change that helps to make our world a better place for all.

—Cicely Lewis, Executive Editor

TABLE OF CONTENTS

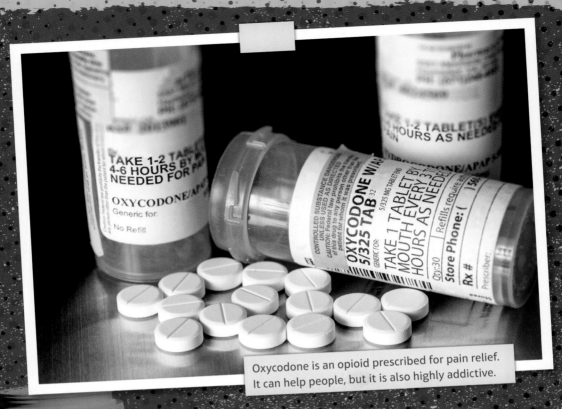

Oxycodone is an opioid prescribed for pain relief. It can help people, but it is also highly addictive.

BACK ON TRACK

OVERCOMING OPIOID ADDICTION IS DIFFICULT. But it is not impossible. More than 40 percent of people who receive medication as part of a treatment recover. Through compassionate, effective treatments, people can overcome their addictions.

When Cortney was sixteen, she was given a prescription opioid pill by a friend. She quickly became addicted and used any money she had to buy pills. Soon she had dropped out of school. After three years of struggling with addiction, she had a breakthrough with the help of recovery programs and counseling. She began to work as an advocate to help others dealing with opioid addiction.

"Thanks to recovery resources and wonderful support from peers and counselors, I realized that I didn't have to live that way anymore," Cortney said. "I realized recovery really was possible for me."

Breaking an opioid addiction can be difficult even if you're world famous. Rapper Eminem struggled with prescription drug addiction for years. His fame gave him more access to pills. But he decided to get clean for his children.

Eminem talks openly about his recovery from addiction to try to help others who are struggling.

Many people who struggle with addiction are able to make a full recovery.

After going through a full rehab program, Eminem recovered. He's stayed drug-free for more than a decade. Every year on the anniversary of his sobriety, he posts on social media about it to inspire others.

"It's been a learning process," he said. "I'm growing. I couldn't believe that anybody could be naturally happy without being on something. So, I would say to anybody, 'It does get better.'"

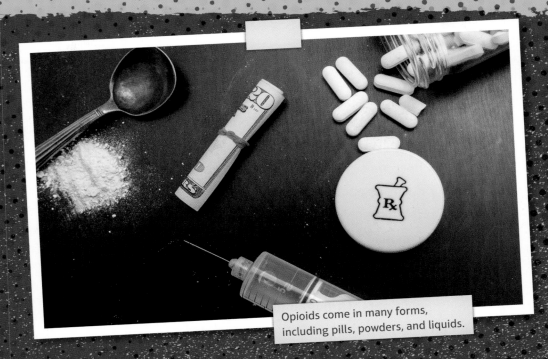

Opioids come in many forms, including pills, powders, and liquids.

CHAPTER 1
WHAT ARE OPIOIDS?

OPIOIDS ARE CHEMICALS THAT INTERACT WITH NERVE CELLS IN THE BODY AND BRAIN. They can produce feelings of euphoria and reduce the intensity and feeling of pain. When used carefully and for a short period, they can provide needed relief by reducing moderate to severe pain.

There are several types of opioids. Medications such as oxycodone and codeine are prescribed by doctors to patients who experience pain. Synthetic opioids such as fentanyl are extremely powerful. And heroin is an illegal opioid.

Opioids, even those prescribed by doctors, can cause harm. In as little as a week, people can become dependent on opioids to reproduce feelings of euphoria. They may take unnecessary pills or search for illegal opioids to reduce pain. They can become sick if they stop taking opioids. Taking stronger doses of opioids increases the risk of overdose (when someone takes too much of a drug at once). An opioid overdose can lead to death.

The word *opioid* comes from the name of the opium poppy plant. Some prescription opioids, such as morphine, are made from poppy plants. Throughout history, people have valued opium for its medicinal and mind-altering effects, and it

An opium poppy plant in bloom

An illustration shows people burning British warehouses in China during the Second Opium War.

has served as a source of conflict. Disputes over the opium trade in Asia led to the Opium Wars (1839–1842, 1856–1860) between Britain and China.

Opioids have been in the US for hundreds of years. Opium dens, places where people could take the drug for pleasure, became popular in the American West in the 1850s. Morphine was given to injured soldiers in the Civil War (1861–1865). Some drug manufacturers even put heroin in children's cough medicine.

RAT PARK

In the late 1970s psychologist Bruce Alexander created the Rat Park study. He gave groups of rats two drinking options: plain water and water with morphine. Rats that lived alone repeatedly drank the morphine water and developed addictions. But the rats that lived in a community with lots of toys and other rats drank the morphine water less and didn't develop addictions as often. The study showed that environment and support can reduce the likelihood of addiction.

Throughout the history of opioid use, addiction has been a major problem. How do people get addicted to these drugs?

When people take opioids, it changes the chemicals in their brains. Opioids can replace their natural endorphins, chemicals that cause feelings of well-being. Their bodies may stop producing enough endorphins to work normally. If they stop taking the opioids, they may experience symptoms of an illness called withdrawal. They may start taking opioids regularly and in stronger doses to avoid withdrawal. Some people turn to illegal drugs, which are often stronger and easier to access. That increases the risk of harm and long-term addiction. It is a difficult cycle to break.

"This problem won't get better overnight."

—Dr. Andrew Kolodny, codirector of opioid policy research, Brandeis University

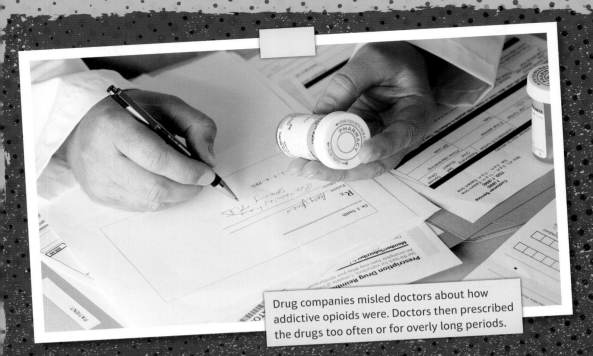

Drug companies misled doctors about how addictive opioids were. Doctors then prescribed the drugs too often or for overly long periods.

CHAPTER 2
NATIONWIDE WORRY

THE UNITED STATES' PROBLEM WITH OPIOIDS HAS ACCELERATED OVER THE PAST TWENTY YEARS. Almost 450,000 people died from opioid overdose from 1999–2018. As the crisis worsened in recent years, an average of 128 people died from overdoses per day.

Several factors caused this crisis. One is that US doctors overprescribed opioids, writing between 150 million and 250 million prescriptions for opioids each year. The daily opioid use rate in the US is one daily dose for every twenty people, much higher than in other countries. People in the US take twenty thousand more daily doses of opioids than those in

Canada, the country with the second-highest usage rate.

"We still prescribe over 80 percent of the world's opioids to less than 5 percent of the world's population," US surgeon general Jerome Adams said in 2018.

The amount of opioids available leads to several issues. When doctors prescribe months' instead of days' worth of pills, patients can take too many and become addicted. Sometimes children, adult relatives, or friends of patients find and use extra pills. Sometimes these pills are sold illegally to drug dealers. Some doctors prescribed and sold opioids to patients who didn't need them. These so-called pill mills helped to spread opioids across the country.

Addiction can happen when people who begin taking opioids for pain become dependent on them to feel good.

THE WAR ON DRUGS

The War on Drugs began with Richard Nixon's presidency (1969–1974) and was escalated through the 1980s and 1990s. During this time, politicians who wanted to appear tough on crime pushed for increasingly harsh punishments for drug possession and use. Because of systemic racism in law enforcement, these punishments fell disproportionately on Black and Latino people. This response to drug use was different from the response to the opioid epidemic. The differences suggest that when white people use drugs, they get information and help. But when Black and Latino people use drugs, they are seen as criminals.

In a 1971 speech, Nixon claimed that drug use was the biggest danger facing the US.

Federal agents raid a so-called pill mill in Florida in 2011. Pill mills give out large amounts of pills with little oversight, contributing to high rates of addiction.

But as the number of pills began to decrease due to government raids of pill mills and stricter prescription laws, use of synthetic opioids, such as fentanyl, began to rise. Fentanyl is fifty to one hundred times stronger than morphine. It is often combined with other drugs, such as cocaine. Many users unknowingly take amounts that can lead to an overdose.

The Appalachian region has been hit hard by the opioid crisis. In places such as Ohio and West Virginia, overdose rates were 48 percent higher than in the rest of the country. In these places, additional factors may have worsened the epidemic. Poverty and a lack of economic opportunities likely contributed to opioid misuse. Poor access to health care

REFLECT

Why do you think doctors and pharmacists gave out so many opioid pills? How might medical professionals help with the current crisis?

and treatment made it difficult for people to treat pain without opioids and to get help with their addictions.

While public attention has focused primarily on white people affected by addiction, the opioid problem crosses racial and ethnic lines. Rates of death from synthetic opioids increased among all races from 2013 to 2017, but they increased more for Black and Latino Americans than white Americans.

The Appalachian region suffered high rates of addiction and overdose in the height of the crisis.

Children are especially vulnerable to the impacts of the opioid crisis.

CHAPTER 3
THE TOLL ON KIDS

OFTEN LEFT OUT OF DISCUSSIONS ABOUT OPIOID ADDICTION IS ITS IMPACT ON CHILDREN. In 2017 more than 2 million children had a parent dealing with opioid use disorder, or had opioid issues themselves. More than 300,000 had been placed into foster care. More than 200,000 had had a parent die. And 170,000 children either accidentally or purposefully took opioids. If current trends continue, the number of children dealing with opioid use disorder could reach 4.2 million by 2030.

Caregivers are often not equipped to support children dealing with opioid issues. Children who have been exposed to

If a parent struggling with addiction is unable to care for their child, a grandparent may step in.

opioid addiction at home can suffer from long-term effects of trauma. Some states are running out of resources to care for children in need.

"It's a cycle of poverty, drug use, and poor health outcomes," said Dr. Elizabeth Coté, chief health officer of the National Institute for Children's Health Quality. "Far too often, those children become the victims of this troubling cycle."

The opioid crisis has put children across the country at risk. In 2019 West Virginia had the highest number of children affected at fifty-four per one thousand kids. But the problem is just as critical in other places. In one school in Philadelphia, teachers speak with children daily about what is happening at home and in their neighborhoods. It gives kids a chance to express their emotions and shows teachers which of their students may need more support.

Educating children about the dangers of opioids at a young age is critical. Research shows that teenagers and young adults often underestimate risk, so they might not understand how easy it is to become addicted. From 2005 to 2020, the use of opioids by teens and young adults has increased rapidly. One in five report misusing opioids. Because their brains are still developing, they can be prone to risky behavior and misuse of opioids.

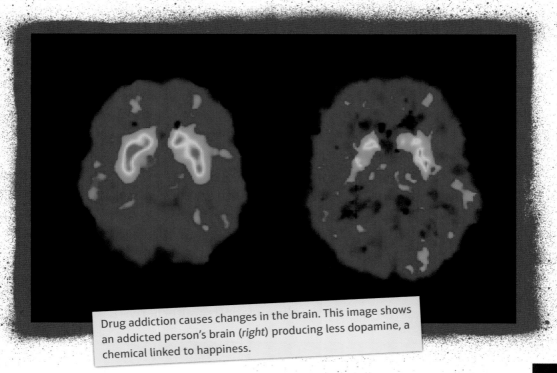

Drug addiction causes changes in the brain. This image shows an addicted person's brain (*right*) producing less dopamine, a chemical linked to happiness.

Activists protest outside the Purdue Pharma headquarters in Stamford, Connecticut, in 2019. Purdue Pharma is owned by the Sackler family, who grew incredibly rich selling opioids.

CHAPTER 4
HELPING HANDS

PEOPLE FROM ALL WALKS OF LIFE HAVE JOINED FORCES TO SOLVE THE OPIOID CRISIS. Organizations across the country lobby for better laws and money for treatment. Fed Up! is a coalition of groups that wants the federal government to pass laws and enact regulations to help end the epidemic. The organization has marched in Washington, DC, several times for the cause.

The medical profession is working on the issue as well. Doctors have tried to limit their prescription of opioids. Having honest conversations with patients about pain can help to determine if other medication or alternative treatments can be used. Some doctors and pharmacists take additional courses to learn more about the effects of opioid use. Many are using databases to check whether patients have already received opioid medications.

Some US cities and counties filed federal lawsuits against opioid manufacturers for the damage the drugs have caused. In 2020 four companies agreed to settle for $26 billion in damages. It was the second-largest federal court case in American history. The money will go to states and local communities that promise to use the funds to assist opioid treatment programs. But those promises are not guaranteed. Other large settlement funds, such as one against the tobacco

Support groups can be helpful for people struggling with addiction.

industry, have been spent by states on programs other than tobacco use prevention.

Public health professionals have embraced the use of medication-assisted treatment (MAT). MAT combines medications with counseling and behavioral therapy to approach opioid misuse. MAT uses medicines such as methadone, buprenorphine, and naltrexone to help with long-term addiction. Another medicine, naloxone, is used to reverse opioid overdoses.

Naloxone training is becoming more available around the US. The drug can save people from overdoses.

> "We have to step in as a society and provide the infrastructure that can help make it more likely that they will succeed."

—Travis Rieder, bioethicist and formerly addicted to opioids

Some critics argue that treating drug addiction with other drugs doesn't make sense. But research shows MAT works better to suppress cravings and block the effects of opioids than treatments without medication. People who receive MAT are less likely to return to using opioids and less likely to die from an opioid overdose. That's why MAT has been approved by organizations such as the National Institute on Drug Abuse.

The opioid crisis is far from over. But people at every level of society are working together to help change the outlook.

REFLECT

What are some steps our government can take to help those with opioid addiction?

TAKE ACTION

Here are some ways you and your family can help with the opioid crisis.

Ask your local representative what your state is doing about the opioid crisis.

Write to your representative to advocate for more widespread access to overdose-fighting drugs such as Narcan in public spaces such as libraries.

Talk to your parents about safely disposing of or returning extra medication.

Consider teaming up with an adult to become a foster care volunteer.

With an adult's permission, donate to an organization fighting the opioid epidemic, such as http://themarahproject.org.

Research the signs of addiction to be prepared to help a friend or family member.

Hold a clothes, diaper, or toy drive for local organizations and hospitals that help babies and children affected by the opioid epidemic.

TIMELINE

3400 BCE: The opium poppy plant is cultivated in lower Mesopotamia and is passed to various cultures.

1803: Friedrich Sertürner, a German scientist, discovers how to create morphine from poppies.

1839: The First Opium War between Britain and China begins.

1895: The Bayer Company, a pharmaceutical company, creates a new product, heroin.

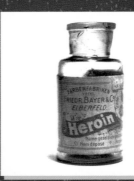

1970: The US passes the Controlled Substances Act, which creates categories for levels of potential abuse.

1995: Purdue Pharma introduces OxyContin, claiming it is safer than other opioids.

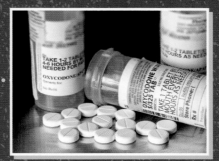

2007: Purdue Pharma pleads guilty for falsely claiming OxyContin is safer than other opioids. The company must pay more than $600 million in fines.

2019: The CDC announces that overdose deaths dropped 5.1 percent in 2018, the first drop in more than two decades.

2020: Oregon becomes the first state to remove criminal penalties for the possession of small amounts of heroin.

GLOSSARY

addiction: an urge to do something that is hard to control or stop

advocate: one who helps the cause of another

compassionate: caring about others

damages: money to be paid as compensation for an injury or loss

endorphin: a chemical in the brain that produces feelings of pleasure and helps the body function

euphoria: a feeling of great happiness and excitement

overdose: taking too much of a drug at once

settlement: a payment that a court of law requires someone to make

synthetic: produced artificially by chemical means

trauma: a scary or dangerous event

withdrawal: an illness caused by stopping the use of a drug

SOURCE NOTES

5   "Cortney," Centers for Disease Control and Prevention, September 22, 2017, https://www.cdc.gov/rxawareness /stories/cortney.html.

6   James Montgomery, "Eminem Details Depths of Drug Addiction: 'My Bottom Was Gonna Be Death,'" MTV, June 27, 2013, http://www.mtv.com/news/1709712/eminem-how-to -make-money-selling-drugs-documentary/.

11   Emma Newburger, "White House Touts Progress in Opioid Crisis, but Health Researchers Are Skeptical," CNBC, March 26, 2019, https://www.cnbc.com/2019/03/26/white-house-touts -progress-in-opioid-crisis-but-some-are-skeptical.html.

13   "U.S. Surgeon General Discusses the Opioid Epidemic," Doctors Company, October 2018, https://www.thedoctors.com/articles /u.s.-surgeon-general-discusses-the-opioid-epidemic/.

18   "Treating the Opioid Epidemic as a Children's Health Crisis," National Institute for Children's Health Quality, accessed February 22, 2021, https://www.nichq.org/insight/treating -opioid-epidemic-childrens-health-crisis/.

23   Stacy Weiner, "A Bioethicist's Personal Opioid Nightmare," AAMC, October 29, 2020, https://www.aamc.org/news-insights /bioethicist-s-personal-opioid-nightmare/.

READ WOKE READING LIST

Goldsmith, Connie. *Addiction and Overdose: Confronting an American Crisis*. Minneapolis: Twenty-First Century Books, 2018.

Hyde, Natalie. *Opioid Crisis*. New York: Crabtree, 2019.

Klimchuk, David. *The Dangers of Opioids*. New York: PowerKids, 2020.

National Prescription Drug Take Back Day
https://takebackday.dea.gov

Sheff, David, and Nic Sheff. *High: Everything You Want to Know about Drugs, Alcohol, and Addiction*. Boston: Houghton Mifflin Harcourt, 2018.

Sirko, Quincy, Clayton Russell, and Angelina Dioguardi. *What the Heck Is Opioid Addiction?* Sewickley, PA: Grow a Generation, 2018.

What You Need to Know about Drugs
https://kidshealth.org/en/kids/know-drugs.html

INDEX

PHOTO ACKNOWLEDGMENTS

Image credits: Steve Heap/Shutterstock.com, pp. 4, 27; AP Photo/ Amy Harris/Invision, p. 5; Thomas Barwick/Getty Images, p. 6; karenfoleyphotography/Shutterstock.com, p. 7; S.G.Photographic/ Shutterstock.com, p. 8; North Wind Picture Archives/Alamy Stock Photo, pp. 9, 26; fotografixx/Getty Images, p. 10; Sean Russell/Getty Images, p. 12; Milko/Getty Images, p. 13; Everett Collection Historical/Alamy Stock Photo, p. 14; AP Photo/Carline Jean/South Florida Sun-Sentinel, p. 15; Sean Pavone/Shutterstock.com, p. 16; Kamira/Shutterstock.com, p. 17; Monkey Business Images/Shutterstock.com, p. 18; Science History Images/Alamy Stock Photo, p. 19; ZUMA Press, Inc./Alamy Stock Photo, p. 20; Roman Chazov/Shutterstock.com, p. 21; New2me86/Shutterstock.com, p. 22; © Mpv_51, p. 26. Cecily Lewis portrait photos by Fernando Decillis.

Design elements: David Smart/Shutterstock.com; Alisara Zilch/ Shutterstock.com; Reddavebatcave/Shutterstock.com.

Cover image: David Smart/Shutterstock.com.

Content consultant: Colin Planalp, senior research fellow at the University of Minnesota's State Health Access Data Assistance Center (SHADAC)

Lerner Publications Company
An imprint of Lerner Publishing Group, Inc.
241 First Avenue North
Minneapolis, MN 55401 USA

For reading levels and more information, look up this title at www.lernerbooks.com.

Main body text set in Aptifer Sans LT Pro.
Typeface provided by Linotype AG.

Designer: Viet Chu **Lerner team:** Martha Kranes

Library of Congress Cataloging-in-Publication Data

Names: Smith, Elliott, 1976– author.
Title: The opioid epidemic and the addiction crisis / Elliott Smith.
Description: Minneapolis : Lerner Publications, 2022 | Series: Issues in action (Read Woke Books) | Includes bibliographical references and index. | Audience: Ages 9–14 | Audience: Grades 7–9 | Summary: "This engaging and informative title delves into the history of the opioid crisis, details the science behind opioid addiction, and advises young people on how they can help those in their communities struggling with addiction"— Provided by publisher.
Identifiers: LCCN 2020057137 (print) | LCCN 2020057138 (ebook) | ISBN 9781728423449 (library binding) | ISBN 9781728431383 (paperback) | ISBN 9781728430690 (ebook)
Subjects: LCSH: Opioid abuse—United States—Juvenile literature. | Drug abuse—United States—Juvenile literature. | Opioids—United States—Juvenile literature.
Classification: LCC RC568.O45 S654 2022 (print) | LCC RC568.O45 (ebook) | DDC 362.290973—dc23

LC record available at https://lccn.loc.gov/2020057137
LC ebook record available at https://lccn.loc.gov/2020057138

Manufactured in the United States of America
1-49182-49313-3/30/2021